STROKE RECOVERY
DIET COOKBOOK

Easy To Prepare Recipes for Stroke Patients to Speed Up Recovery

LAKEISHA OWENS

Copyright @ 2024 by LAKEISHA OWENS

All rights reserved. No part of this book may be reproducedin any form or by any electronic or mechanical means,including information storehouse and reclamation systems, without authorization in writing from the publisher, exceptby a critic, who may quote brief passages in a review. Thisbook is a work of non-fiction.

Published in 2024

TABLE OF CONTENT

INTRODUCTION 5

RECIPES 8

BREAKFAST RECIPE 8

Avocado Toast on Whole Grain Bread 8

Egg Muffins with Vegetables 11

Greek Yogurt Parfait 12

Spinach and Feta Omelette 13

Sweet Potato and Black Bean Breakfast Burrito 14

Whole Grain Pancakes with Fruit Compote 15

Salmon and Cream Cheese on Whole Grain Bagel 17

More....................

LUNCH RECIPES 19

Baked Salmon with Steamed Broccoli 19

Turkey and Avocado Wrap 20

Lentil Soup 21

Chicken Avocado Salad 22

Veggie Stir-Fry with Brown Rice 23

Tuna Salad on Whole Grain Bread 24

Sweet Potato Chickpea Buddha Bowl 25

Beet and Goat Cheese Arugula Salad 26

More.............

DINNER RECIPES 29

   Baked Herb Chicken with Roasted Vegetables 29

   Salmon and Asparagus Foil Packs 30

   Vegetable Stir-Fry with Tofu 31

   Simple Baked Cod with Spinach 32

   Grilled Shrimp and Vegetable Kabobs 33

   Turkey Meatballs with Zucchini Noodles 34

   Lentil and Kale Soup 40

   Chicken and Vegetable Soup 41

   Tomato Basil Soup 42

   Broccoli Cheddar Soup 43

   More…………

SNACKS RECIPE 49

   Avocado Toast 49

   Hummus and Veggie Sticks 50

   Almond Butter and Banana Slices 51

   Oatmeal Energy Balls 51

   Cheese and Whole-Grain Crackers 52

   Smoothie with Spinach, Banana, and Almond Milk 52

   Cottage Cheese and Pineapple 53

   Sliced Pear with Ricotta Cheese 54

CONCLUSION 55

   DAILY MEAL PLANNER 57

INTRODUCTION

"Stroke Recovery Diet Cookbook," a comprehensive guide designed to support individuals on their journey to recovery following a stroke. As health professionals deeply immersed in the fields of neurology, nutrition, and rehabilitative care, we understand the critical role that diet plays in healing and overall well-being. This cookbook is the culmination of evidence-based research, clinical expertise, and a heartfelt commitment to aiding those affected by stroke in reclaiming their health and vitality through nutrition.

A stroke can be a life-altering event, affecting physical functioning, emotional health, and everyday activities. Recovery is often a challenging path, marked by significant lifestyle adjustments and rehabilitation. Among these adjustments, diet emerges as a pivotal factor. The right nutrition can not only support the body's repair processes but also improve cardiovascular health, reduce inflammation, and optimize overall recovery outcomes.

Our goal in creating this cookbook is to demystify the concept of a "Stroke Recovery Diet" by providing practical, delicious, and nutritious recipes that cater to the unique needs of stroke survivors. Each recipe has been carefully developed and reviewed by a team of dietitians, therapists, and stroke recovery experts to ensure they are not only beneficial for recovery but also accessible and enjoyable.

In this book, you will find meals rich in antioxidants, fiber, healthy fats, and essential nutrients, all aimed at fostering neurological health, enhancing physical strength, and promoting mental well-being. Whether you are a stroke survivor, caregiver, or a health professional looking to expand your toolkit, this cookbook is designed to offer you a resource that is both scientifically informed and deeply compassionate.

Let this cookbook be your guide and companion on the road to recovery. Through nourishing meals and informed dietary choices, we invite you to experience the healing power of food. Together, let's embark on this journey toward recovery, resilience, and renewed health through what we are eating.

HAPPY COOKING!!!!!!!

BREAKFAST RECIPE

RECIPES

BREAKFAST RECIPE

Avocado Toast on Whole Grain Bread

Top whole grain bread with mashed avocado, a rich source of monounsaturated fats, and a poached egg for protein. Sprinkle some chia seeds for omega-3 fatty acids.

Ingredients:

1 slice whole grain bread

1/2 ripe avocado

1 egg

Pinch of salt and pepper

1 tsp chia seeds

Instructions:

Toast the whole grain bread to your liking.

Mash the avocado and spread it on the toasted bread.

Poach or lightly fry the egg in a non-stick skillet with a little olive oil.

Season with salt and pepper.

Place the egg on top of the mashed avocado.

Sprinkle chia seeds over the top and serve immediately.

Oatmeal with Berries and Nuts

Prepare oatmeal with almond milk and top it with a mix of berries (blueberries, strawberries, raspberries) for antioxidants and walnuts or almonds for healthy fats and a bit of protein.

Ingredients:

1/2 cup rolled oats
1 cup almond milk
1/2 cup mixed berries
1 tbsp walnuts or almonds, chopped
1 tsp honey or maple syrup (optional)

Instructions:

Cook the oats in almond milk according to package instructions.

Once cooked, transfer to a bowl and top with mixed berries and nuts.

Drizzle with honey or maple syrup if desired.

Smoothie Bowl

Blend spinach, a banana, blueberries, flaxseed (for omega-3s), and almond milk until smooth. Pour into a bowl and top with sliced fruits, nuts, and a sprinkle of granola.

Ingredients:

1 cup spinach

1 banana

1/2 cup blueberries

1 tbsp flaxseed

3/4 cup almond milk

Toppings: sliced fruits, nuts, granola

Instructions:

Blend spinach, banana, blueberries, flaxseed, and almond milk until smooth.

Pour into a bowl and top with your choice of sliced fruits, nuts, and granola.

Egg Muffins with Vegetables

Whisk together eggs, diced bell peppers, spinach, and onions. Pour into muffin tins and bake. These can be made in advance and are easy to reheat.

Ingredients:

6 eggs

1/2 cup diced bell peppers

1/2 cup spinach, chopped

1/4 cup onions, diced

Salt and pepper to taste

Instructions:

Preheat the oven to 350°F (175°C) and lightly grease a muffin tin.

Whisk together the eggs, salt, and pepper in a bowl.

Stir in the bell peppers, spinach, and onions.

Pour the mixture into the muffin tins and bake for 20-25 minutes, or until set.

Greek Yogurt Parfait

Layer Greek yogurt (for protein and probiotics) with mixed berries, a drizzle of honey, and granola for a crunchy texture. Add flaxseeds or chia seeds for extra fiber and omega-3s.

Ingredients:

1 cup Greek yogurt

1/2 cup mixed berries

2 tbsp granola

1 tsp honey

1 tbsp flaxseeds or chia seeds

Instructions:

In a glass or bowl, layer Greek yogurt, mixed berries, and granola.

Repeat the layers until all ingredients are used.

Drizzle with honey and sprinkle flaxseeds or chia seeds on top.

Spinach and Feta Omelette

Whisk eggs and cook them in a pan to make an omelet, adding spinach (for iron and folate) and feta cheese. Serve with a slice of whole grain toast for added fiber.

Ingredients:

2 eggs

1/4 cup spinach, chopped

2 tbsp feta cheese, crumbled

Salt and pepper to taste

1 tsp olive oil

Instructions:

Beat the eggs with salt and pepper.

Heat olive oil in a skillet over medium heat.

Add the eggs and cook for a few minutes until they begin to set.

Sprinkle spinach and feta cheese over half of the omelette.

Fold the other half over the filling and continue to cook until the eggs are fully set.

Sweet Potato and Black Bean Breakfast Burrito

Fill a whole grain tortilla with mashed sweet potato, black beans, scrambled eggs, and avocado slices for a hearty, nutritious breakfast rich in fiber and healthy fats.

Ingredients:

1 medium sweet potato, cubed and cooked

1/2 cup black beans, rinsed and drained

2 eggs, scrambled

2 whole grain tortillas

1/4 avocado, sliced

Salt and pepper to taste

Instructions:

Warm the tortillas in a skillet or microwave.

Divide the cooked sweet potato, black beans, scrambled eggs, and avocado slices between the tortillas.

Season with salt and pepper, fold into burritos, and serve.

Whole Grain Pancakes with Fruit Compote

Make pancakes using whole grain flour and top with a compote made from simmered berries and a touch of maple syrup. Serve with a side of Greek yogurt for protein.

Ingredients (Pancakes):

1 cup whole grain flour
1 tbsp sugar (optional)
1 tsp baking powder
1/2 tsp salt
1 egg
1 cup milk
2 tbsp unsalted butter, melted

Ingredients (Compote):

2 cups mixed berries
2 tbsp maple syrup

Instructions:

For the pancakes, mix the dry ingredients in one bowl and the wet ingredients in another.

Combine both, stirring until just mixed.

Cook pancakes on a hot, lightly greased griddle or pan, flipping once bubbles form on top.

For the compote, simmer the berries and maple syrup over medium heat until the berries have softened.

Serve the pancakes with fruit compote on top.

Salmon and Cream Cheese on Whole Grain Bagel

Spread low-fat cream cheese on a whole grain bagel and top with smoked salmon (rich in omega-3 fatty acids), capers, and thinly sliced red onions.

Ingredients:

1 whole grain bagel, halved and toasted
2 tbsp low-fat cream cheese
2 oz smoked salmon
1 tbsp capers
Thinly sliced red onion

Instructions:

Spread the cream cheese evenly on each half of the toasted bagel.

Lay slices of smoked salmon over the cream cheese.

Top with capers and red onion slices before serving.

LUNCH RECIPES

LUNCH RECIPES

Baked Salmon with Steamed Broccoli

Ingredients:

2 salmon fillets (4 oz each)
1 tbsp olive oil
Salt and pepper to taste
1 lemon, sliced
2 cups broccoli florets

Instructions:

Preheat the oven to 400°F (200°C).
Line a baking sheet with parchment paper.
Place salmon fillets on the baking sheet.
Drizzle with olive oil and season with salt and pepper. Top with lemon slices.
Bake for 12-15 minutes or until salmon is cooked through.
Steam the broccoli florets until tender, about 5 minutes.
Serve alongside the salmon.

Turkey and Avocado Wrap

Ingredients:

2 whole grain tortillas

4 slices turkey breast

1 ripe avocado, sliced

1/2 cup spinach leaves

1/4 cup shredded carrot

2 tbsp hummus

Instructions:

Spread 1 tablespoon of hummus on each tortilla.

Layer turkey slices, avocado slices, spinach leaves, and shredded carrot on top of the hummus.

Roll up the tortillas tightly, cut in half, and serve.

Lentil Soup

Ingredients:

1 cup dried lentils, rinsed
1 onion, diced
2 carrots, diced
2 stalks celery, diced
2 cloves garlic, minced
4 cups vegetable broth
1 tsp ground cumin
Salt and pepper to taste
2 tbsp olive oil

Instructions:

In a large pot, heat the olive oil over medium heat. Add the onion, carrots, celery, and garlic. Sauté until softened, about 5 minutes. Add the lentils, vegetable broth, cumin, salt, and pepper. Bring to a boil, then reduce heat and simmer, covered, for 25-30 minutes, or until lentils are tender. Serve hot, optionally garnished with fresh parsley or a squeeze of lemon.

Chicken Avocado Salad

Ingredients:

2 cups cooked chicken breast, shredded

1 ripe avocado, diced

1/2 cup cherry tomatoes, halved

1/4 red onion, thinly sliced

2 tbsp Greek yogurt

1 tbsp lemon juice

Salt and pepper to taste

1 tbsp fresh cilantro, chopped

Instructions:

In a large bowl, combine the chicken, avocado, cherry tomatoes, and red onion.

In a small bowl, mix the Greek yogurt, lemon juice, salt, and pepper.

Pour over the chicken mixture and toss to coat evenly.

Garnish with chopped cilantro before serving.

Veggie Stir-Fry with Brown Rice

Ingredients:

2 cups mixed vegetables (bell peppers, broccoli, snap peas)
1 tbsp olive oil
2 cloves garlic, minced
1 tbsp soy sauce (low sodium)
1 tsp ginger, grated
1 cup cooked brown rice

Instructions:

Heat the olive oil in a large pan over medium-high heat.

Add the garlic and ginger, sautéing for about 30 seconds.

Add the mixed vegetables and stir-fry until tender-crisp, about 5-7 minutes.

Stir in the soy sauce and cook for another minute.

Serve the stir-fried vegetables over cooked brown rice.

Tuna Salad on Whole Grain Bread

Ingredients:

1 can (5 oz) tuna in water, drained

2 tbsp Greek yogurt

1/4 cup diced celery

1/4 cup diced apple

Salt and pepper to taste

4 slices whole grain bread

Lettuce leaves

Instructions:

In a bowl, mix the tuna, Greek yogurt, celery, apple, salt, and pepper.

Place lettuce leaves on two slices of bread, top with the tuna mixture, then cover with the remaining slices of bread.

Cut in half and serve.

Sweet Potato Chickpea Buddha Bowl

Ingredients:

1 medium sweet potato, cubed
1 cup chickpeas, drained and rinsed
2 cups spinach leaves
1/2 avocado, sliced
2 tbsp olive oil
Salt and pepper to taste
1 tbsp tahini
1 tbsp lemon juice

Instructions:

Preheat the oven to 400°F (200°C).

Toss sweet potato cubes with 1 tablespoon olive oil, salt, and pepper. Roast for 20-25 minutes, or until tender.

In a bowl, arrange the roasted sweet potato, chickpeas, spinach, and avocado slices.

Drizzle with tahini, the remaining olive oil, and lemon juice before serving.

Beet and Goat Cheese Arugula Salad

Ingredients:

2 medium beets, roasted, peeled, and sliced

2 cups arugula

1/4 cup goat cheese, crumbled

1/4 cup walnuts, toasted and chopped

2 tablespoons balsamic vinegar

1 tablespoon extra-virgin olive oil

1 teaspoon honey (optional)

Salt and pepper to taste

1/4 cup sliced red onion (optional)

Instructions:

Wrap beets in foil and roast at 400°F until tender, about 45-60 minutes. Cool, peel, and slice.

Toast walnuts in the oven until fragrant, about 5-10 minutes. Let cool, then chop.

Whisk balsamic vinegar, olive oil, honey, salt, and pepper in a bowl.

In a large bowl, combine arugula, sliced beets, optional red onion, crumbled goat cheese, and toasted walnuts.

Drizzle with the dressing and gently toss to combine.

Enjoy immediately for the best flavor and texture.

DINNER RECIPE

DINNER RECIPES

Baked Herb Chicken with Roasted Vegetables

Ingredients:

2 chicken breasts

1 tbsp olive oil

1 tsp rosemary, thyme, and oregano (each)

Salt and pepper to taste

1 cup mixed vegetables (carrots, Brussels sprouts, sweet potatoes), cubed

Instructions:

Preheat oven to 375°F (190°C).

Season chicken with herbs, salt, pepper, and olive oil. Place in a baking dish.

Toss vegetables with olive oil, salt, and pepper. Spread around the chicken.

Bake for 25-30 minutes, until chicken is cooked and vegetables are tender.

Salmon and Asparagus Foil Packs

Ingredients:

2 salmon fillets

1 bunch asparagus, trimmed

2 tbsp olive oil

Lemon slices

Salt and pepper to taste

Instructions:

Preheat oven to 400°F (200°C).

Cut two sheets of foil, place salmon and asparagus on each.

Drizzle with olive oil, add lemon slices, and season.

Fold foil over and seal edges. Bake for 20 minutes, or until salmon is cooked through.

Vegetable Stir-Fry with Tofu

Ingredients:

1 block firm tofu, cubed
2 cups mixed vegetables (broccoli, bell peppers, snap peas)
2 tbsp soy sauce (low sodium)
1 tbsp sesame oil
1 garlic clove, minced
1 tsp ginger, minced

Instructions:

Heat sesame oil in a pan over medium heat. Add garlic and ginger; sauté for 1 minute.

Add tofu and cook until golden on all sides.

Add vegetables and soy sauce. Stir-fry until vegetables are just tender.

Serve over brown rice or quinoa.

Simple Baked Cod with Spinach

Ingredients:

2 cod fillets

2 cups fresh spinach

1 tbsp olive oil

Lemon slices

Salt and pepper to taste

Instructions:

Preheat oven to 400°F (200°C).

Place cod on a baking sheet, season with salt, pepper, and olive oil. Surround with spinach and lemon slices.

Bake for 12-15 minutes, until cod is cooked through and spinach is wilted.

Grilled Shrimp and Vegetable Kabobs

Ingredients:

1 lb. shrimp, peeled and deveined
2 bell peppers, cut into pieces
1 zucchini, sliced
1 onion, cut into wedges
2 tbsp olive oil
1 lemon, juiced
Salt and pepper to taste

Instructions:

Preheat grill to medium-high.

Thread shrimp and vegetables onto skewers. Drizzle with olive oil, lemon juice, salt, and pepper.

Grill for 5-7 minutes on each side, until shrimp is cooked and vegetables are tender.

Turkey Meatballs with Zucchini Noodles

Ingredients:

1 lb. ground turkey

1 egg

1/4 cup breadcrumbs

1 tsp garlic powder

1 tsp Italian seasoning

Salt and pepper to taste

2 zucchinis, spiralized

Instructions:

Preheat oven to 375°F (190°C).

Mix turkey, egg, breadcrumbs, spices, salt, and pepper. Form into meatballs.

Place meatballs on a baking sheet. Bake for 20-25 minutes.

Serve over zucchini noodles with your favorite sauce.

Cauliflower Fried Rice

Ingredients:

1 head cauliflower, grated into "rice"
1 cup mixed vegetables (peas, carrots, corn)
2 eggs, beaten
2 tbsp soy sauce (low sodium)
1 tbsp sesame oil
1 garlic clove, minced

Instructions:

Heat sesame oil in a large pan.

Add garlic and sauté for 1 minute.

Add cauliflower rice and vegetables.

Cook for 5-7 minutes.

Push rice to the side, add eggs, and scramble.

Mix everything together.

Stir in soy sauce and serve.

Chickpea and Spinach Curry

Ingredients:

1 can chickpeas, drained and rinsed

1 onion, diced

2 cups spinach

1 can coconut milk

2 tbsp curry powder

Salt to taste

1 tbsp olive oil

Instructions:

Heat olive oil in a pot.

Add onion and cook until soft.

Add chickpeas, curry powder, and salt. Cook for a few minutes.

Add coconut milk and bring to a simmer.

Stir in spinach until wilted.

Serve with brown rice or naan.

SOUP RECIPE

Carrot Ginger Soup

Ingredients:

1 tbsp olive oil
1 onion, chopped
2 cloves garlic, minced
2 tbsp fresh ginger, grated
1-pound carrots, peeled and diced
4 cups vegetable broth
Salt and pepper to taste

Instructions:

In a large pot, heat olive oil over medium heat. Add onion and garlic, cooking until softened.

Stir in ginger and carrots. Cook for a few minutes until fragrant.

Add vegetable broth, bring to a boil, then simmer until carrots are tender, about 20 minutes.

Puree soup using an immersion blender until smooth. Season with salt and pepper.

Lentil and Kale Soup

Ingredients:

1 tbsp olive oil

1 onion, diced

2 carrots, diced

2 stalks celery, diced

2 cloves garlic, minced

1 cup lentils, rinsed

6 cups vegetable broth

2 cups kale, chopped

Salt and pepper to taste

Instructions:

Heat olive oil in a large pot over medium heat.

Add onion, carrots, and celery, sautéing until softened.

Add garlic and lentils, cooking for another minute.

Pour in vegetable broth and bring to a boil.

Reduce heat and simmer until lentils are tender, about 25 minutes.

Stir in kale and cook until wilted.

Season with salt and pepper.

Chicken and Vegetable Soup

Ingredients:

1 tbsp olive oil
1 onion, chopped
2 carrots, sliced
2 stalks celery, sliced
2 cloves garlic, minced
1 pound chicken breast, cubed
6 cups chicken broth
2 cups mixed vegetables (peas, corn, green beans)
Salt and pepper to taste

Instructions:

In a large pot, heat olive oil over medium heat.

Add onion, carrots, celery, and garlic, sautéing until vegetables are softened.

Add chicken and cook until no longer pink.

Pour in chicken broth and bring to a boil.

Reduce heat and simmer until chicken is cooked through, about 15 minutes.

Add mixed vegetables and cook for another 5-10 minutes.

Season with salt and pepper.

Tomato Basil Soup

Ingredients:

1 tbsp olive oil

1 onion, diced

2 cloves garlic, minced

1 can (28 oz) whole tomatoes

2 cups vegetable broth

1/4 cup fresh basil, chopped

Salt and pepper to taste

Instructions:

Heat olive oil in a large pot over medium heat.

Add onion and garlic, cooking until softened.

Add whole tomatoes (with juice) and vegetable broth.

Bring to a boil, then simmer for 20 minutes.

Use an immersion blender to puree the soup until smooth.

Stir in chopped basil and season with salt and pepper.

Broccoli Cheddar Soup

Ingredients:

1 tbsp olive oil

1 onion, chopped

2 cloves garlic, minced

4 cups broccoli florets

3 cups vegetable broth

1 cup cheddar cheese, grated

1 cup milk

Salt and pepper to taste

Instructions:

In a large pot, heat olive oil over medium heat.

Add onion and garlic, cooking until softened.

Add broccoli and vegetable broth.

Bring to a boil, then simmer until broccoli is tender, about 15 minutes.

Stir in cheddar cheese until melted, then pour in milk.

Puree soup with an immersion blender to desired consistency.

Season with salt and pepper.

Sweet Potato and Coconut Soup

Ingredients:

1 tbsp olive oil

1 onion, diced

2 cloves garlic, minced

2 large sweet potatoes, peeled and cubed

1 can (14 oz) coconut milk

4 cups vegetable broth

Salt and pepper to taste

1 tsp curry powder (optional)

Instructions:

Heat olive oil in a large pot over medium heat.

Add onion and garlic, cooking until softened.

Add sweet potatoes, coconut milk, vegetable broth, and curry powder if using.

Bring to a boil, then simmer until sweet potatoes are tender, about 20 minutes.

Puree the soup with an immersion blender until smooth.

Season with salt and pepper.

Pea and Mint Soup

Ingredients:

1 tbsp olive oil

1 onion, diced

2 cups frozen peas

4 cups vegetable broth

1/4 cup fresh mint leaves

Salt and pepper to taste

Instructions:

Heat olive oil in a large pot over medium heat.

Add onion, cooking until softened.

Add peas and vegetable broth. Bring to a boil, then simmer for 10 minutes.

Stir in mint leaves, then puree the soup with an immersion blender until smooth.

Season with salt and pepper.

Butternut Squash Soup

Ingredients:

1 tbsp olive oil

1 onion, diced

1 butternut squash, peeled, seeded, and cubed

4 cups vegetable broth

Salt and pepper to taste

1 tsp nutmeg

Instructions:

Heat olive oil in a large pot over medium heat.

Add onion, cooking until softened.

Add butternut squash and vegetable broth.

Bring to a boil, then simmer until squash is tender, about 20 minutes.

Puree the soup until smooth. Season with salt, pepper, and nutmeg.

Miso Soup with Tofu and Seaweed

Ingredients:

4 cups water
2 tbsp miso paste
1/2 cup tofu, cubed
1/4 cup seaweed, chopped (e.g., wakame)
2 green onions, sliced
A few slices of fresh ginger (optional)

Instructions:

Bring the water to a simmer in a pot.

If using, add the ginger slices to the water for a few minutes to infuse it with flavor, then remove them.

In a small bowl, dissolve the miso paste in a little bit of the hot water from the pot to make it easier to mix.

Add the dissolved miso back to the pot, keeping the water at a low simmer.

Miso should not boil, as high heat can destroy its beneficial probiotics.

Add the tofu and seaweed to the pot and cook gently for about 3-5 minutes, until the tofu is heated through and the seaweed is rehydrated.

Turn off the heat and add the sliced green onions just before serving.

SNACKS RECIPE

SNACKS RECIPE

Avocado Toast

Ingredients:

Whole-grain bread

1 ripe avocado

Lemon juice

Salt and pepper

Red pepper flakes (optional)

Instructions:

Toast the bread to your liking.

Mash the avocado in a bowl, add a squeeze of lemon juice, and season with salt and pepper.

Spread the mashed avocado on the toast.

Sprinkle with red pepper flakes for an extra kick if desired.

Greek Yogurt and Berries

Ingredients:

Greek yogurt

Mixed berries (strawberries, blueberries, raspberries)

A drizzle of honey (optional)

Instructions:

Scoop Greek yogurt into a bowl.

Top with fresh or frozen mixed berries.

Drizzle with honey for a touch of sweetness if desired.

Hummus and Veggie Sticks

Ingredients:

Hummus

Carrot sticks

Cucumber slices

Bell pepper strips

Instructions:

Prepare a variety of vegetable sticks.

Serve with a side of hummus for dipping.

Almond Butter and Banana Slices

Ingredients:

Almond butter

1 banana

Instructions:

Slice the banana.

Spread almond butter on each slice.

Oatmeal Energy Balls

Ingredients:

1 cup rolled oats

1/2 cup almond butter

1/4 cup honey

1/4 cup dark chocolate chips

1/4 cup dried cranberries

Instructions:

Mix all ingredients in a bowl until well combined.

Roll the mixture into small balls.

Refrigerate for at least an hour before serving.

Cheese and Whole-Grain Crackers

Ingredients:

Slices of cheese (choose low-sodium options)

Whole-grain crackers

Instructions:

Pair slices of cheese with whole-grain crackers for a balanced snack.

Smoothie with Spinach, Banana, and Almond Milk

Ingredients:

1 banana

A handful of spinach

1 cup almond milk

Ice cubes (optional)

Instructions:

Blend all ingredients until smooth.

Add ice cubes for a colder drink if desired.

Roasted Chickpeas

Ingredients:

1 can chickpeas, drained and rinsed

1 tablespoon olive oil

Seasonings of choice (paprika, garlic powder, salt)

Instructions:

Preheat oven to 400°F (200°C).

Toss chickpeas with olive oil and seasonings.

Spread on a baking sheet and roast for 20-30 minutes until crispy.

Cottage Cheese and Pineapple

Ingredients:

Cottage cheese

Fresh pineapple chunks

Instructions:

Serve a scoop of cottage cheese with a side of fresh pineapple chunks.

Sliced Pear with Ricotta Cheese

Ingredients:

1 pear, sliced

Ricotta cheese

A drizzle of honey (optional)

Cinnamon (optional)

Instructions:

Spread ricotta cheese on pear slices.

Drizzle with honey and sprinkle with cinnamon if desired.

Conclusion

In crafting "The Stroke Recovery Diet Cookbook," we've embarked on a journey through the realms of nutrition and culinary delight, all tailored to support the intricate path of healing and rehabilitation after a stroke. This collection of breakfasts, lunches, dinners, soups, and snacks is not merely a compilation of recipes but a testament to the power of food as medicine and comfort.

Each recipe has been meticulously designed with the stroke survivor in mind, prioritizing ingredients that are known to aid in reducing inflammation, lowering blood pressure, improving heart health, and fostering overall well-being. From the nutrient-rich breakfasts that kickstart the day with energy and optimism, to the comforting and hearty dinners that conclude the day with satisfaction and nourishment, every meal serves a purpose beyond mere sustenance. They are stepping stones on the path to recovery.

The lunches and soups offer versatility and convenience, acknowledging the varying appetites and abilities of stroke survivors. They are crafted to be both easy to prepare and consume, ensuring that the act of eating remains a pleasure, not a challenge. The snacks provide quick, nutritious options to maintain energy levels and support a healthy metabolism throughout the day.

As we conclude this culinary journey, let us reflect on the power of food to heal, comfort, and bring joy. The recipes in this book are more than just meals; they are a form of therapy, a celebration of life, and a source of hope. They underscore the belief that recovery is not only about regaining what was lost but also discovering new strengths, tastes, and pleasures.

May "Stroke Recovery Diet Cookbook" serve as a constant companion in your recovery journey, offering nourishment for both the body and soul. Here's to a journey filled with flavorful discoveries and small victories at the dining table, each contributing to a larger triumph over stroke's challenges.

DAILY MEAL PLANNER

DAILY MEAL PLANNER

DAY _____

BREAKFAST

_____

_____

LUNCH

_____

_____

DINNER

_____

_____

INGREDIENTS NEEDED

☐ _____

☐ _____

☐ _____

DAILY MEAL PLANNER

DAY _____

BREAKFAST
_____
_____

LUNCH
_____
_____

DINNER
_____
_____

INGREDIENTS NEEDED

☐ _____
☐ _____
☐ _____

DAILY MEAL PLANNER

DAY _____

BREAKFAST

_____
_____

LUNCH

_____
_____

DINNER

_____
_____

INGREDIENTS NEEDED

☐ _____
☐ _____
☐ _____

DAILY MEAL PLANNER

DAY _____

BREAKFAST

_____
_____

LUNCH

_____
_____

DINNER

_____
_____

INGREDIENTS NEEDED

☐ _____
☐ _____
☐ _____

DAILY MEAL PLANNER

DAY _____

BREAKFAST

_____
_____

LUNCH

_____
_____

DINNER

_____
_____

INGREDIENTS NEEDED

☐ _____
☐ _____
☐ _____

DAILY MEAL PLANNER

DAY _____

BREAKFAST

_____
_____

LUNCH

_____
_____

DINNER

_____
_____

INGREDIENTS NEEDED

- [ ] _____
- [ ] _____
- [ ] _____

DAILY MEAL PLANNER

DAY _____

BREAKFAST
_____
_____

LUNCH
_____
_____

DINNER
_____
_____

INGREDIENTS NEEDED

☐ _____
☐ _____
☐ _____

DAILY MEAL PLANNER

DAY _____

BREAKFAST
_____
_____

LUNCH
_____
_____

DINNER
_____
_____

INGREDIENTS NEEDED

☐ _____
☐ _____
☐ _____

DAILY MEAL PLANNER

DAY _____

BREAKFAST

_____
_____

LUNCH

_____
_____

DINNER

_____
_____

INGREDIENTS NEEDED

☐ _____
☐ _____
☐ _____

DAILY MEAL PLANNER

DAY _____

BREAKFAST

_____
_____

LUNCH

_____
_____

DINNER

_____
_____

INGREDIENTS NEEDED

☐ _____
☐ _____
☐ _____

DAILY MEAL PLANNER

DAY _____

BREAKFAST
_____
_____

LUNCH
_____
_____

DINNER
_____
_____

INGREDIENTS NEEDED

☐ _____
☐ _____
☐ _____

DAILY MEAL PLANNER

DAY _____

BREAKFAST
_____
_____

LUNCH
_____
_____

DINNER
_____
_____

INGREDIENTS NEEDED

- [ ] _____
- [ ] _____
- [ ] _____

DAILY MEAL PLANNER

DAY _____

BREAKFAST
_____
_____

LUNCH
_____
_____

DINNER
_____
_____

INGREDIENTS NEEDED

☐ _____
☐ _____
☐ _____

DAILY MEAL PLANNER

DAY _____

BREAKFAST

_____
_____

LUNCH

_____
_____

DINNER

_____
_____

INGREDIENTS NEEDED

☐ _____
☐ _____
☐ _____

DAILY MEAL PLANNER

DAY _____

BREAKFAST

_____

_____

LUNCH

_____

_____

DINNER

_____

_____

INGREDIENTS NEEDED

☐ _____

☐ _____

☐ _____

DAILY MEAL PLANNER

DAY _____

BREAKFAST

_____
_____

LUNCH

_____
_____

DINNER

_____
_____

INGREDIENTS NEEDED

☐ _____
☐ _____
☐ _____

DAILY MEAL PLANNER

DAY _____

BREAKFAST

_____
_____

LUNCH

_____
_____

DINNER

_____
_____

INGREDIENTS NEEDED

☐ _____
☐ _____
☐ _____

DAILY MEAL PLANNER

DAY _____

BREAKFAST

_____
_____

LUNCH

_____
_____

DINNER

_____
_____

INGREDIENTS NEEDED

☐ _____
☐ _____
☐ _____

DAILY MEAL PLANNER

DAY _____

BREAKFAST
_____
_____

LUNCH
_____
_____

DINNER
_____
_____

INGREDIENTS NEEDED

☐ _____
☐ _____
☐ _____

DAILY MEAL PLANNER

DAY _____

BREAKFAST
_____
_____

LUNCH
_____
_____

DINNER
_____
_____

INGREDIENTS NEEDED

☐ _____
☐ _____
☐ _____

DAILY MEAL PLANNER

DAY _____

BREAKFAST

_____
_____

LUNCH

_____
_____

DINNER

_____
_____

INGREDIENTS NEEDED

☐ _____
☐ _____
☐ _____

DAILY MEAL PLANNER

DAY _____

BREAKFAST

_____
_____

LUNCH

_____
_____

DINNER

_____
_____

INGREDIENTS NEEDED

- ☐ _____
- ☐ _____
- ☐ _____

DAILY MEAL PLANNER

DAY _____

BREAKFAST

_____
_____

LUNCH

_____
_____

DINNER

_____
_____

INGREDIENTS NEEDED

☐ _____
☐ _____
☐ _____

DAILY MEAL PLANNER

DAY _____

BREAKFAST
_____
_____

LUNCH
_____
_____

DINNER
_____
_____

INGREDIENTS NEEDED

☐ _____
☐ _____
☐ _____

DAILY MEAL PLANNER

DAY _____

BREAKFAST
_____
_____

LUNCH
_____
_____

DINNER
_____
_____

INGREDIENTS NEEDED

☐ _____
☐ _____
☐ _____

DAILY MEAL PLANNER

DAY _____

BREAKFAST
_____
_____

LUNCH
_____
_____

DINNER
_____
_____

INGREDIENTS NEEDED

☐ _____
☐ _____
☐ _____

DAILY MEAL PLANNER

DAY _____

BREAKFAST
_____
_____

LUNCH
_____
_____

DINNER
_____
_____

INGREDIENTS NEEDED

☐ _____
☐ _____
☐ _____

DAILY MEAL PLANNER

DAY _____

BREAKFAST
_____
_____

LUNCH
_____
_____

DINNER
_____
_____

INGREDIENTS NEEDED

☐ _____
☐ _____
☐ _____

DAILY MEAL PLANNER

DAY _____

BREAKFAST
_____
_____

LUNCH
_____
_____

DINNER
_____
_____

INGREDIENTS NEEDED

☐ _____
☐ _____
☐ _____

DAILY MEAL PLANNER

DAY _____

BREAKFAST

_____

_____

LUNCH

_____

_____

DINNER

_____

_____

INGREDIENTS NEEDED

☐ _____

☐ _____

☐ _____

Printed in Great Britain
by Amazon